FANTASY BASKETBALL MATH

USING STATS TO SCORE BIG IN YOUR LEAGUE

BY MATT DOEDEN

CAPSTONE PRESS
a capstone imprint

Sports Illustrated Kids Fantasy Sports Math is published by Capstone Press,
1710 Roe Crest Drive, North Mankato, Minnesota 56003.
www.mycapstone.com

Library of Congress Cataloging-in-Publication Data
Names: Doeden, Matt.
Title: Fantasy basketball math : using stats to score big in your league / by Matt Doeden.
Description: Mankato, Minnesota : Capstone Press, [2017] | Series: Sports Illustrated Kids.
   Fantasy Sports Math | Includes bibliographical references and index. | Audience: Ages:
   8-12. | Audience: Grades: 4 to 6. | Description based on print version record and CIP
   data provided by publisher; resource not viewed.
Identifiers: LCCN 2015051397 (print) | LCCN 2015049423 (ebook) | ISBN 9781515721635
   (library binding) | ISBN 9781515721734 (eBook PDF)
Subjects: LCSH: Fantasy basketball (Game)—Mathematical models—Juvenile literature.
Classification: LCC GV1202.F333 (print) | LCC GV1202.F333 D64 2017 (ebook) |
   DDC 793.93001/5118—dc23
LC record available at http://lccn.loc.gov/2015051397

Summary: Describes how to use statistics and math to create and run a successful fantasy
basketball team.

Editorial Credits
Aaron Sautter, editor; Sarah Bennett, designer; Eric Gohl, media researcher;
Katy LaVigne, production specialist

Photo Credits
Newscom: EPA/Larry W. Smith, 4-5, EPA/Tannen Maury, 16, USA Today Sports/Dan Hamilton, 26-27,
USA Today Sports/Jerome Miron, 24; Shutterstock: EKS, 2-3; Sports Illustrated: Al Tielemans, cover,
Andy Hayt, 25, David E. Klutho, 17, 22-23, John Biever, 10-11, John W. McDonough, 6-7, 9, 12-13, 14,
20, 21, 28-29, Robert Beck, 8, Simon Bruty, 18-19

Design Elements: Shutterstock

Printed and bound in the United States of America.
009678F16

TABLE OF CONTENTS

BRINGING THE EXCITEMENT 5

CHAPTER 1
SCORING WITH STATS..............6

CHAPTER 2
TYPES OF LEAGUES.................12

CHAPTER 3
DRAFT DAY............................18

CHAPTER 4
PLAY BALL!
MANAGING YOUR TEAM.........22

GLOSSARY..........................30
READ MORE.......................... 31
INTERNET SITES..................... 31
INDEX 32

Kevin Durant ⇒

BRINGING THE EXCITEMENT

You hold your breath as the Oklahoma City Thunder's Kevin Durant slices through the lane. You rise to your feet when LeBron James throws down a monster dunk for the Cleveland Cavaliers. Then you shout in celebration when your team comes out on top. Welcome to the thrilling world of fantasy basketball!

National Basketball Association (NBA) games are packed with excitement. But fantasy basketball creates a way to make the action even more exciting. You can build and run your own team of NBA stars in a fantasy league. Their performance and the numbers they rack up will determine whether you win or lose. Fantasy sports are all about **statistics**. Knowing the game of basketball and its players is a good start. However, if you want to dominate your league, you'll need to know the math too.

statistics—numbers, facts, or other data collected about a specific subject

CHAPTER 1

SCORING WITH STATS

There's no single way to keep score in fantasy basketball. Each league sets up its own scoring system. But they all have one thing in common—it's all about the stats.

The Core Stats

Almost all fantasy basketball leagues use a few **core stats**. Points, rebounds, assists, steals, blocks, and three-pointers are fairly simple. You just add them up to get a total. But field goal percentage and free-throw percentage are a little trickier. You'll need to do a little more math to figure them out.

Suppose Los Angeles Clippers center DeAndre Jordan takes 20 shots at the basket and makes 12 of them. To figure out his field goal percentage, first divide his total shots made by his total shots taken.

$$12 \div 20 = 0.60$$

Next, take that number and multiply by 100 to get Jordan's percentage:

$$.60 \times 100 = 60.0 \text{ percent}$$

The same math determines a player's free throw percentage. Suppose the Golden State Warriors' Klay Thompson takes ten free throw shots and makes eight of them. Using the above process, what is his free throw percentage? Check your answer at the bottom of the next page.

DeAndre Jordan

core stats—the basic stats used by most fantasy basketball leagues; they include points, rebounds, assists, steals, blocks, three-pointers, field goal percentage, and free-throw percentage

Point Scoring

Many fantasy basketball leagues keep score with a basic point-based system. Every stat is worth a point value. In a point-based system, each point, rebound, assist, steal, block, and 3-pointer made is normally worth 1 point. You just add them up to get a single total. Suppose you have L.A. Clippers forward Blake Griffin on your team. Check out his stat line for one game. How many fantasy points did he earn for you? Check your answer below.

Blake Griffin: 25 points, 11 rebounds, 2 assists, 1 steal, 1 block, 0 three-pointers

⇑ Blake Griffin

Answer: 25 + 11 + 2 + 1 + 1 + 0 = 40 fantasy points

Some fantasy players think this basic system focuses too much on a player's scoring ability. So they award extra points for other stats. For example, rebounds might be worth 1.5 points. Assists could be worth 2 points each. Steals, blocks, and three-pointers could each count for 3 points. Now how many points would Griffin have if you include bonus points? Look below to see if you have the right answer.

Knowing how your league breaks down points will determine which players you'll want on your team.

Kobe Bryant

FANTASY POINT EXPLOSION

Kobe Bryant, Los Angeles Lakers

January 22, 2006
- 81 points
- 6 rebounds
- 2 assists
- 3 steals
- 1 block
- 7 three-pointers

Total Basic Fantasy Points = 100

Answer: 25 (points) + 16.5 (rebounds) + 4 (assists) + 3 (steals) + 3 (blocks) + 0 (3-pointers) = 51.5 fantasy points

Category Scoring

Point-based leagues are simple and easy to learn. But many fantasy players crave something deeper. In category scoring there's no single fantasy point total. Fantasy players instead compete to win in several stat categories. A basic category system might use the eight core stats as eight categories. The goal is to have the highest total in as many categories as possible.

For example, take a look at the following results in a **head-to-head league**. How many categories would you win?

	POINTS	REBOUNDS	ASSISTS	STEALS	BLOCKS	3-POINTERS	FG%	FT%
You	311	99	47	30	22	20	45%	87%
Opponent	422	96	44	29	22	31	47%	81%

You won four categories—rebounds, assists, steals, and free-throw percentage. Your opponent won in points, 3-pointers, and field goal percentage. The two teams tied in blocks. Congrats! Your team just notched a victory, 4–3–1. These figures are then added to your team's total wins, losses, and ties. The team with the best overall record at the end of the season is the winner.

head-to-head league—a league that pits teams directly against each other, usually in a weekly format

FANTASY POINT *EXPLOSION*

Kevin Love, Minnesota Timberwolves

November 12, 2010
- 35 points
- 31 rebounds
- 5 assists
- 1 block
- 1 three-pointer

Total Basic Fantasy Points = 73

← Kevin Love

CHAPTER 2

TYPES OF LEAGUES

There are many types of fantasy basketball leagues that players can join. Head-to-head (H2H) leagues are the most common. But there are several others to pick from.

Banging Heads

Do you love straight-up, one-on-one competition? Then a head-to-head league might be for you. For a week at a time, it's just you vs. your opponent. H2H leagues can use either category-based or point-based scoring. The type used can make a huge difference. Imagine getting the following results:

	POINTS	REBOUNDS	ASSISTS	STEALS	BLOCKS	3-POINTERS
You	100	50	20	10	5	10
Opponent	89	30	22	12	7	11

In a basic point-based league, you crushed it. Add up the stat points and you grabbed a 195–171 victory. But what happens if you're in a category-based league? How did you do? Do the math and see if you're right with the answer at the bottom.

Answer: In a category-based league, you lost 4–2.

← Klay Thompson

FANTASY POINT *EXPLOSION*

Stephen Curry, Golden State Warriors

February 27, 2013
54 points
6 rebounds
7 assists
3 steals
11 three-pointers
Total Basic Fantasy Points = 81

Stephen Curry

Rotisserie Leagues

If you prefer tracking stats over the long haul, then a rotisserie, or roto, league might be for you. In roto leagues you compete against your entire league over a whole season. Teams earn rankings in each category. In a ten-team league, if you finish first in any category, you'll score 10 points. Last place is worth just 1 point.

But beware. Roto leagues aren't for casual players. They require a lot of sorting, adding, and tracking. Until you know how it works, it can be confusing. Let's keep it simple for now. Imagine a tiny three-team league that uses only the points and rebounds categories. Finishing first in any category is worth 3 points. Second place is worth 2, and third is worth 1.

	POINTS	REBOUNDS
Wily Wildcats	8,111	3,701
Bruising Bears	9,014	3,033
Super Shooters	7,900	3,159

Which team is the winner? First, rank the teams for each category to figure out their point totals. In points the Bruising Bears finish in first, so they get 3 points. The Wily Wildcats are second and get 2 points. The Super Shooters come in last to get 1 point. For rebounds, it's Wily Wildcats first (3 points), Super Shooters second (2 points), and Bruising Bears third (1 point).

Now add the rankings up. The Wily Wildcats come out on top with a total of 5 points. The Bruising Bears finish with 4 points, and the Super Shooters get 3 points. Now imagine how much math is involved for a 12-team league using 10 different stat categories!

FANTASY FACT

Balance is the key in roto leagues. You don't have to actually win any categories to be the league champion. The secret is to try not to finish near the bottom in many categories.

rotisserie—a type of fantasy league in which stats are added throughout a season and owners are awarded points according to their rankings in each category

Dynasty Leagues

If you're a die-hard basketball fan, you might want to try a **dynasty league**. These leagues allow owners to keep at least some players from year to year. They also often use a **salary cap** to make sure teams stay balanced. You need to carefully consider which players to keep on your team. It's a big decision. Let go of the wrong player and you might regret it for years.

Suppose you've already decided to keep Cleveland Cavaliers forward Kevin Love. You get to keep one more player for your team. Who do you choose? You need to weigh all the factors before deciding.

	POSITION	SALARY	AGE	PROJECTED FANTASY POINTS
Jabari Parker, Milwaukee Bucks	guard	$10	20	25 per game
Tim Duncan, San Antonio Spurs	center	$14	39	30 per game
Carmelo Anthony, New York Knicks	forward	$36	31	44 per game

Jabari Parker

Carmelo Anthony

Tim Duncan is a great value. But he's 39 years old. He might not play much longer. Carmelo Anthony looks like the best player. But he's also the most expensive, and you've already kept one forward. Jabari Parker is the least productive. But he's young and cheap. He's also likely to get better over time. There's no right or wrong answer here. To make the best decision, you have to crunch the numbers and know what type of scoring system your league uses.

dynasty league—a type of fantasy league in which owners keep some of their players from year to year

salary cap—a limit of the total amount of money that can be spent on a team's players; salary caps are normally used in auction-style fantasy leagues

CHAPTER 3

DRAFT DAY

Draft day! It's the biggest day in any fantasy season. It's where you build your team and begin putting your strategy to work. Let's see how you can draft a championship team.

The Snake

Fantasy basketball leagues commonly use snake drafts. These are done in rounds. Each team owner takes turns picking players to fill out his team. The draft order flips each round. So if you pick last in Round 1, you'll be first in Round 2. Here's how the first two rounds would look in a typical snake draft.

ROUND	TEAM 1	TEAM 2	TEAM 3	TEAM 4	TEAM 5	TEAM 6	TEAM 7	TEAM 8	TEAM 9	TEAM 10
1	Pick 1	Pick 2	Pick 3	Pick 4	Pick 5	Pick 6	Pick 7	Pick 8	Pick 9	Pick 10
2	Pick 20	Pick 19	Pick 18	Pick 17	Pick 16	Pick 15	Pick 14	Pick 13	Pick 12	Pick 11

Drafting a good team is all about **projections**. These are your best guesses on how each player will perform. Say you have the following players at the top of your draft list. Try ranking their value based on their stats. Add up the rows to get a projection of points per game for each player. Which player should you target with your draft pick? Check your answer on the next page.

	POINTS	REBOUNDS	ASSISTS	STEALS	BLOCKS	3-POINTERS
John Wall, Washington Wizards	17	4	10	2	0	1
Damian Lillard, Portland Trail Blazers	25	5	6	1	0	2
DeMarcus Cousins, Sacramento Kings	24	13	4	1	2	0

18   projection—an estimate of a player's possible statistics

John Wall ⇓

Auction Drafts

Going once, going twice … SOLD! Many fantasy players think auction drafts provide the real fun in fantasy sports. In these drafts each owner gets a fixed amount of money to spend, often $200. It's not real cash. But you still need a **budget** for spending it.

Suppose you need to fill 13 **roster** spots for your team. What is the average amount of money you can spend on each player? Check your answer below.

Of course, you won't actually spend the same amount on every player. A superstar may cost you $50, $60, or more. Let's say you shell out $55 for the Houston Rockets' James Harden. Then you get a little wild and spend $60 on New Orleans Pelicans forward Anthony Davis. You've already spent $115 of your money. Now you've got just $85 left and 11 more players to draft. You'll have to do some serious bargain hunting to complete your team.

budget—a plan for spending money

roster—all of the players on a team

Answer: $200 ÷ 13 = $15.40

TIERS

One key to a successful auction draft is to use **tiers**. These are groups of players that are expected to perform at a similar level. You can make your own tiers based on player rankings. Or you can use tiers found on fantasy basketball Internet sites. Let's say that the Indiana Pacers' Paul George, the Utah Jazz's Gordon Hayward, and the Phoenix Suns' Eric Bledsoe are all expected to get similar stats. They're all in the same tier. Suppose George and Bledsoe each go for $30 in your auction. If you can get Hayward for $20, that's a bargain. You'd be getting a valuable player for less money. That leaves you extra cash to spend on another good player later. By paying attention to tiers, you can get the most bang for your buck.

tier—a group of players at one position who are projected to score similar point totals

21

CHAPTER 4

PLAY BALL!

MANAGING YOUR TEAM

The draft is over. It's time to relax and enjoy the season, right? Nope. Now it's time to manage your team. The most basic task you'll have is to set your starting roster. Some leagues let you adjust your starters day by day. Others lock your roster in for an entire week.

Checking Matchups

Matchups are key to figuring out who to start. Good fantasy owners track opposing teams' defenses when choosing their starters. Imagine that you need to start one of your small forwards. Which player gives you the best chance to score the most points?

	AVG POINTS SCORED	OPPONENT	AVG POINTS ALLOWED TO SMALL FORWARDS
Kawhi Leonard, San Antonio Spurs	39 points/game	Cleveland	29 points/game
Jimmy Butler, Chicago Bulls	34 points/game	Denver	38 points/game

Leonard has been the better fantasy scorer. But Cleveland plays tough defense. To create a point projection for Leonard, add his average to Cleveland's defensive average: 39 + 29 = 68. Then divide that number by two: 68 ÷ 2 = 34 fantasy points for Leonard. Now do the same for Butler. How many projected fantasy points can you expect from him? Do the math and check your answer below.

Answer: (34 + 38) ÷ 2 = 36 fantasy points. Butler would be the better player to start.

Jimmy Butler ⇧

23

Transaction Time

The fantasy draft is where you build your core team. But you can't stop there. To keep your team on top, you'll need to make **transactions** during the season. Managing your team will include adding players, dropping players, and making trades.

Things change fast in the NBA. Players get hurt. Others simply don't perform well. You'll probably need to drop a few of your players at some point. You should also keep up on who's hot. You may want to grab them before someone else does.

Wesley Matthews ⇒

transaction—a change on a team's roster, such as adding or dropping a player, or making a trade

Suppose you're in a weekly point-based H2H format. Your starter, Minnesota Timberwolves guard Andrew Wiggins, has the flu and isn't expected to play for a few days. You need to grab a replacement quick. The following players are available:

PLAYER	AVG FANTASY POINTS/GAME	GAMES IN SCORING PERIOD
DeMar DeRozan, Toronto Raptors	28	3
Kyle Korver, Atlanta Hawks	22	4
Wesley Matthews, Dallas Mavericks	17	5

Which player is projected to score the most for the week? Multiply their fantasy average by the number of games they'll play to find out. Look below to see if you got the correct answer.

FANTASY POINT *EXPLOSION*

Michael Jordan, Chicago Bulls

March 28, 1990
  69 points
  18 rebounds
  6 assists
  4 steals
  1 block
  2 three-pointers
Total Fantasy Points = 100

Answer: DeRozan = 84 points; Korver = 88 points; Matthews = 85 points. The smart money is on Korver. You should grab him while you can.

The Trading Block

Let's make a deal! You might love the players you drafted and don't want to give them up. After all, you picked them for a reason. But it's smart not to overlook one of the most exciting parts of fantasy basketball—the trading block. Wheeling and dealing your players can help transform a good team into a champion.

Imagine another owner sends you this offer:

YOU GIVE UP	POSITION	AVG FANTASY POINTS/GAME
Anthony Davis, New Orleans Pelicans	Center	50
Rudy Gay, Sacramento Kings	Guard	22

YOU GET IN RETURN		
Marc Gasol, Memphis Grizzlies	Center	39
Kyle Lowry, Toronto Raptors	Guard	35

Many fantasy owners can't bear to trade away big stars like Davis. But you've still got to look at the numbers. Gasol and Lowry combine for an average 74 fantasy points per game. Davis and Gay put up 72. Do you stick with your elite player? Or do you add depth to your team to fuel a possible championship run? The decision could make or break your season.

← Kyle Lowry

FANTASY POINT *EXPLOSION*

LeBron James, Miami Heat

March 3, 2014
  61 points
  7 rebounds
  4 assists
  9 three-pointers
Total Fantasy Points = 81

Crushing Your League with Math

You may never get the chance to hit a game-winning shot in the NBA Finals. But don't let that stop you. Playing fantasy basketball can help you learn more about the game. It can make you feel closer to your favorite players. You'll even cheer on players you might otherwise overlook. Fantasy basketball can also help you become more familiar with the entire league.

But knowing the NBA and its players is only half the story. To achieve fantasy glory, you also need to master the math. You need to know how the stats work and how to use them to your advantage. So sit down and practice crunching the numbers. Before long you'll have the math skills you need to dominate your league.

GLOSSARY

budget (BUH-juht)—a plan for spending money

core stats (KOHR STATZ)—main statistical categories used by most fantasy basketball leagues; these include points scored, rebounds, assists, steals, blocks, three-pointers, field goal percentage, and free throw percentage

head-to-head league (HED-to-HED LEEG)—a league that pits teams directly against each other, usually in a weekly format

projection (pruh-JEK-shuhn)—an estimate of a player's possible statistics

roster (ROS-tur)—a list of players on a team

rotisserie league (roh-TISS-uh-ree LEEG)—a type of fantasy league in which stats are added throughout a season; owners are awarded points according to their rankings in each category

dynasty league (DIE-nuh-stee LEEG)—a type of fantasy league in which owners keep some of their players from year to year

salary cap (SAL-uh-ree KAP)—a limit of the total amount of money that can be spent on a team's players

statistics (stuh-TISS-tiks)—numbers, facts, or other data collected about a specific subject

tier (TEER)—a group of players at one position who are expected to score similar point totals

transaction (tran-ZAK-shuhn)—a change on a team's roster, such as adding or dropping a player, or making a trade

READ MORE

Braun, Eric. *Basketball Stats and the Stories Behind Them: What Every Fan Needs to Know.* Sports Stats and Stories. North Mankato, Minn.: Capstone Press, 2016.

Kortemeier, Todd. *Pro Basketball by the Numbers.* Pro Sports by the Numbers. North Mankato, Minn.: Capstone Press, 2016.

Murray, Stuart A. P. *Score with Basketball Math.* Score with Sports Math. Berkeley Heights, N.J.: Enslow Publishers, Inc., 2013.

INTERNET SITES

FactHound offers a safe, fun way to find Internet sites related to this book. All of the sites on FactHound have been researched by our staff.

Here's all you do:

Visit *www.facthound.com*

Type in this code: 9781515721635

Check out projects, games and lots more at
www.capstonekids.com

INDEX

Anthony, Carmelo, 16, 17

Bledsoe, Eric, 21
Bryant, Kobe, 9
Butler, Jimmy, 22

Curry, Stephen, 14

Davis, Anthony, 20, 26
drafting teams, 18, 24
    auction drafts, 20, 21
    player projections, 18
    player tiers, 21
    snake drafts, 18
Duncan, Tim, 17
Durant, Kevin, 5

Gasol, Marc, 26
Gay, Rudy, 26
George, Paul, 21
Griffin, Blake, 8

Harden, James, 20
Hayward, Gordon, 21

James, LeBron, 5, 28
Jordan, DeAndre, 6
Jordan, Michael, 25

league types, 12
    dynasty leagues, 16–17
    head-to-head leagues, 10,
        12, 25
    rotisserie leagues, 15
Leonard, Kawhi, 22
Love, Kevin, 11, 16
Lowry, Kyle, 26

managing your team
    choosing starters, 22
    matchups, 22
    point projections, 22, 25
    trading players, 24, 26
    transactions, 24–25

National Basketball
    Association (NBA), 5, 29

Parker, Jabari, 16, 17

rosters, 20

salary caps, 16
scoring systems, 6, 15, 17
    category-based scoring,
        10, 12
    point-based scoring, 8–9,
        12, 25
statistics, 5, 6, 12, 15, 18, 21, 29
    assists, 6, 8, 9, 10, 12, 18
    blocks, 6, 8, 9, 10, 12, 18
    categories, 10, 12, 15, 18
    field goal percentage, 6, 10
    free-throw percentage, 6, 10
    points, 6, 8, 10, 12, 15, 18
    rebounds, 6, 8, 9, 10, 12, 15, 18
    steals, 6, 8, 9, 10, 12, 18
    three-point shots, 6, 8, 9, 10,
        12, 18

Thompson, Klay, 6

Wiggins, Andrew, 25